CELEBRATING THE FAMILY NAME OF YU

Celebrating the Family Name of Yu

Walter the Educator

Silent King Books
a WhichHead Entertainment Imprint

Copyright © 2024 by Walter the Educator

All rights reserved. No part of this book may be reproduced in any manner whatsoever without written permission except in the case of brief quotations embodied in critical articles and reviews.

First Printing, 2024

Disclaimer

This book is a literary work; the story is not about specific persons, locations, situations, and/or circumstances unless mentioned in a historical context. Any resemblance to real persons, locations, situations, and/or circumstances is coincidental. This book is for entertainment and informational purposes only. The author and publisher offer this information without warranties expressed or implied. No matter the grounds, neither the author nor the publisher will be accountable for any losses, injuries, or other damages caused by the reader's use of this book. The use of this book acknowledges an understanding and acceptance of this disclaimer.

Celebrating the Family Name of Yu is a memory book that belongs to the Celebrating Family Name Book Series by Walter the Educator. Collect them all and more books at WaltertheEducator.com

USE THE EXTRA SPACE TO DOCUMENT YOUR FAMILY MEMORIES THROUGHOUT THE YEARS

YU

Yu, a name like a tranquil stream,

Flowing gently, a timeless dream.

Its path is carved with grace and might,

A family bond, a guiding light.

In ancient scrolls and tales of old,

The Yu name shines like burnished gold.

With wisdom deep and courage true,

It stands the test of all it knew.

Through forests vast and skies so wide,

The Yu name carries strength inside.

A lineage proud, both firm and free,

A testament to legacy.

The bamboo sways, yet never breaks,

A lesson Yu so wisely takes.

Resilient hearts, a steady hand,

Its roots secure in every land.

The Yu name echoes in the breeze,

In songs of birds and rustling trees.

A harmony of love and care,

A timeless gift beyond compare.

In every craft, in every trade,

The Yu name's mark is firmly laid.

A spark of hope, a steady flame,

Its essence strong, its truth the same.

From rising sun to twilight's hue,

The Yu name carries dreams anew.

Through each endeavor, each new start,

It holds its place in every heart.

Like rivers joining endless seas,

The Yu name flows with boundless ease.

Through trials faced and battles won,

Its legacy shines like the sun.

In whispered words and voices loud,

The Yu name stands forever proud.

A family built on trust and grace,

A name that time cannot erase.

So here's to Yu, a name of gold,

A story vast, a spirit bold.

Through every age, in all it's done,

The Yu name shines for everyone.

ABOUT THE CREATOR

Walter the Educator is one of the pseudonyms for Walter Anderson. Formally educated in Chemistry, Business, and Education, he is an educator, an author, a diverse entrepreneur, and he is the son of a disabled war veteran. "Walter the Educator" shares his time between educating and creating. He holds interests and owns several creative projects that entertain, enlighten, enhance, and educate, hoping to inspire and motivate you. Follow, find new works, and stay up to date with Walter the Educator™

at WaltertheEducator.com

www.ingramcontent.com/pod-product-compliance
Lightning Source LLC
LaVergne TN
LVHW052009060526
838201LV00059B/3932